ISBN-13: 9781234567890
ISBN-10: 1477123456

Library of Congress Control Number: 2018675309
Printed in the United States of America

This book is dedicated to endless possibility and productive positivity.

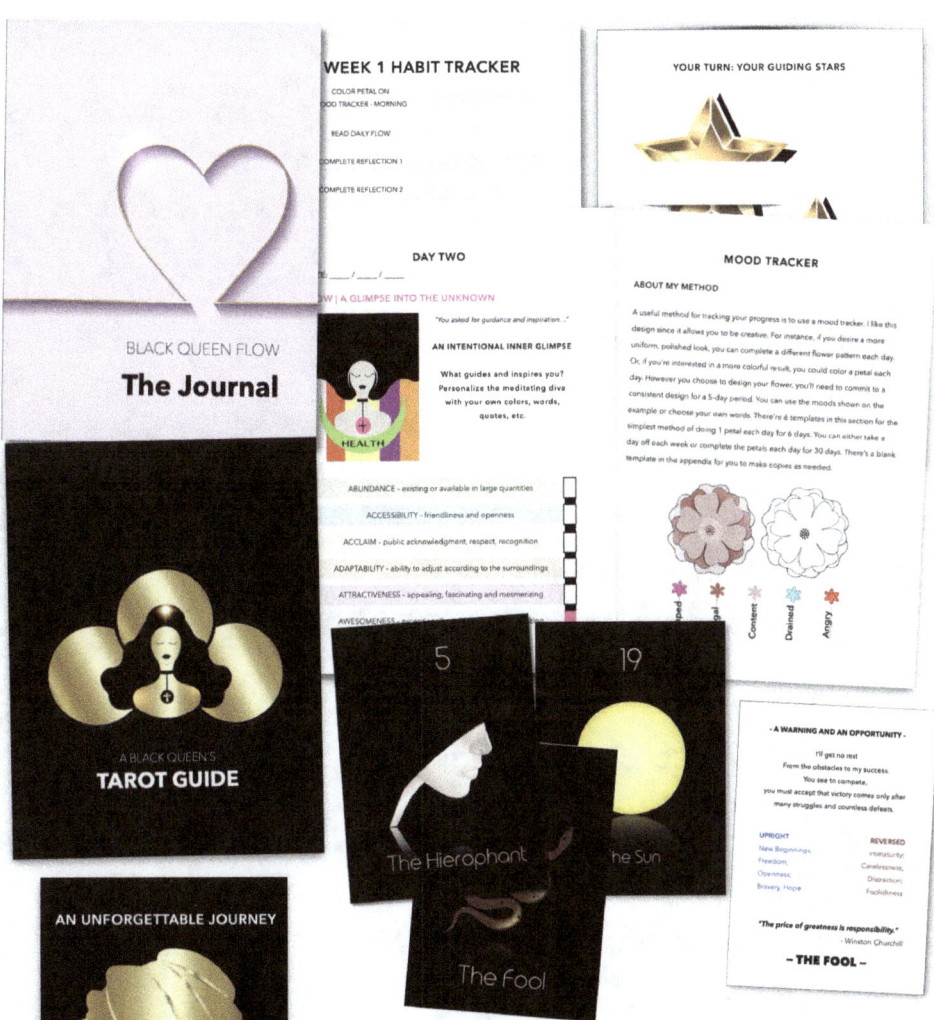

COMPLETE 30-DAY PROGRAM

- **DAILY INSPIRATION**
- **CUSTOM TAROT DECK + GUIDE**
- **CUSTOM JOURNAL**

Table Of Contents

Day 1 | Empathy for the Young Queen

Before me stands a young queen

In the midst of turmoil I too have lived and seen

It tears me apart to see you in such pain

I too hate there's a cost for every gain.

For riches are both a blessing and a

burdensome tether,

This too will get somewhat easier, but not

necessarily fully resolved or better.

Day 2 | The Last Time

You came at me sidewise - wild and unstrung.

I let you vent - I held my tongue.

Pure ignorance - do what you will…

I sit in silence - held my piece still

I let you finish the rant you'd begun

I looked at you coldly - then said "I'm done".

Day 3 | A Glimpse of the Unknown

You asked for guidance and inspiration

To help you see the warnings and other indications.

But, now you feel your hesitation...

To confront the reality of your situation.

You can stay and tolerate the stagnation

Or you can move on to your next destination.

So, do you choose preservation?

Or are you brave enough to chase transformation?

Day 4 | Regret

I watched it burn without regret

So too burned memories I can stand to forget

Was it in vain - just an empty endeavor?

It matters not - it's gone forever.

Day 5 | The Beast Within

Another day, another plight…

Here I stand, once again, prepared to fight.

Decimated the field, until all are crushed.

A dragon, a monster is what they say…

All that's true - I really don't play.

Day 6 | Arise!

Another river to cross
Another soul to reach
More masses to inspire
With another speech

I churn out the words
Turn up the charm
My people are vulnerable
And I need you armed.

My words are simple
Forceful and
direct
We're steady
climbing
But we're not
there yet.

Day 7 | Danger

Though calm and personable, you must beware
Because I don't go out of my way to scare
See, you don't know what my weapons are.
And one step closer may be one step too far.
This is the only warning you'll get.
Trust me, love, you ain't seen nothing like me
yet.

Day 8 | Bring It

A darkness surrounds you and stains your heart,

You've earned nothing; yet consider yourself

smart.

I'm scarred, weary and yet

You'll still need every last troop you get

For between you and this triumph stands my

will

And that's something you'll never kill.

Day 9 | Confrontation

So quick to turn - by Satan led
Yeah, you messed up - I heard what you said.
So keep your distance - Don't come near.
Unless you're looking for trouble, that's right here.
I suggest you keep it moving - just pass on through.
We both know what's coming for you.

Day 10 | The Devil - Reversed

Hater, enemy, acquaintance, "friend"

You refuse to accept that you'll never win.

The misery you wish for me is the one you live in.

Meanwhile I'm more at peace than I've ever

been.

Day 11 | Power Trip

Do you see this as a sanctuary or a cage?

I see what I fear and what I crave.

A refuge, an illusion, an extension of the stage

Another tool to mediate the gaze

Power within the inscrutability of a sage

So, is this as a sanctuary or a cage?

Day 12 | Black Queen Magic

I speak the truth

I can devastate with a look.

I laugh at what's mistook

about the power of this smooth hook

        And the things it attracts

Like the envy of those who lack

So damn scared of my clap-back

        When they see me they step back

So fierce my awesome impact

This Black
Queen Magic -
they can't
counteract.

Day 13 | Motivation

I'm used to this now - I'll face whatever you bring.

No longer concerned with making this pleasing...

Too busy relishing my season.

An outsider who fought her way to the in and wasn't too particular about the way.

With a reputation so fearsome, no one sees me as easy prey.

When I spit, I thrill and set hearts afire

Inspiring my people and myself to reach even higher.

Day 14 | Victory for the Weary

I'll get no rest...

From the obstacles to my success.

You see to compete...

You must accept that victory comes only after

many struggles and countless defeats.

Day 15 | I've Been Changed - Verse 3

I know I've been changed

I only tolerate your ridiculousness

Because it occurs as I'm minding my

business

Simply put, I don't have time for you or your

games.

Like I said, I know I've been changed.

Day 16 | I've Been Changed - Verse 4

I know I've been changed

Because I no longer feel a daily rage

I've calmed down as I've mastered the game

Sometimes I even relish the challenges

posed by my reign...

Like I said, I know I've been changed.

Day 17 | Is This What You Want?

To the few, the chosen, the legacy
Assume the platform of responsibility
For afterwards you must be mindful and graceful in
all that you do
Mess this up and another chance may not be
offered to you...

Day 18 |
Real Talk

We face more
discrimination
So, I take care with my
presentation
Since there's higher
expectations.
That means...
I'm twice as good
And not too hood
So I can stack max cash
And can make it last.

Day 19 | Celebrity

You smile, wave and play to the crowds

As the haters whisper and scowl furiously typing

things they dare not say aloud.

The cheers, the jeers - it all comes to you

You could dispute each lie;

but, what good will it do?

To see you thriving just rips at their hearts

So they'll do anything to tear you apart

Oh that you have the nerve to be beautiful, talented

and smart!

Day 20 | I've Been Changed - Verse 5

I know I've been changed

I earn all these hard gains

And I endure all the strains.

I break free of all chains.

I'm the master of my domain.

Like I said, I know I've been changed.

Day 21 | Making It

She knows she'll ultimately win.
Sacrificed too much to give in.
She works hard to get things
to where they
need to be.
The toll it takes
isn't for others to
see.
She's self-
possessed
because that's
how she survives
So, does it matter
if she feels like it's
a disguise
sometimes?

Day 22 | You Don't Wanna Blow It

This world can be
scary place
and you know it.
But, go in blind
and you'll to blow
it.
You'd better hurry
up and use that
head
before you get
horribly misled.

Day 23 | I Know I've Been Changed - Verse 1

I know that I've been changed

By the relentless grind

My beauty now shines.

I survived all the flames.

After all that pain -

I won't ever be the same…

Like I said, I know that I've changed.

Day 24 | Dropped

It was fun at times; but, I'm ending this today.

Simply put, I've decided to go my own way.

So, do what you do - say what you say...

I'm done with you anyway.

Day 25 | I've Been Changed - Verse 6

I've been changed.

What stands before you are just the remains

I know you don't recognize me - I should look

strange.

By all mess I overcame,

Like I said, I know I been changed.

So close to ideal

A union is so powerful that it seems unreal

In you I find a serenity - an opportunity to rest;

A place where I don't have to shine as the brightest

and best.

I'm me unfiltered - effervescent and blessed.

Day 27 | Decay

When one problem persists, other problems take root...

Then the mind shrivels slowly like dehydrated fruit.

Witnessing the beauty of God's child in the midst of decay,

Smashes you heart and brutally rips the fabric of normalcy away.

You can watch stoically, tearfully, or even slip away.

Choose carefully though - that could be you someday.

Day 28 | You Don't Get It

I said I'm a queen
Do you know what
that means?
It means that I don't
have time to waste
on you
You still down there
and baby I done
flew
So, it's not my fault
if this crown is out
of your view
You standing still but I'm on a breakthrough
But you just go wherever the winds may blow
You're so small-minded it makes sense you don't
know
How to process this black queen's flow.

Day 29 | Forbidden Fruit

My path you've attempted to trace
And crept into my circle janus-faced
No, I won't give you even a taste
It'll make it too difficult for you to know your place
You've come to this here - unwanted and unbidden
To taste this sweet fruit; but, that's forbidden

Day 30 | Secret Sauce

Some try so hard to keep me back

They convince themselves I couldn't be *all* that

Then stand mystified as I lap them on life's track

Weeping from my vicious wisecracks

Wanting to know my life hack

My secret they just can't crack

I'm majestic because I'm black

www.ingramcontent.com/pod-product-compliance
Lightning Source LLC
Chambersburg PA
CBHW060358130626
46553CB00003B/1287